Loving Large
Daily Readings

Loving Large
Daily Readings

Jacob Armstrong

Abingdon Press
Nashville

LOVING LARGE: DAILY READINGS
by Jacob Armstrong

Copyright © 2013 by Abingdon Press
All rights reserved.

This book is printed on acid-free, elemental chlorine-free paper.

Library of Congress Cataloging-in-Publication applied for.

ISBN 978-1-4267-7378-5

13 14 15 16 17 18 19 20 21 22—10 9 8 7 6 5 4 3 2 1

MANUFACTURED IN THE UNITED STATES OF AMERICA

Contents

Introduction

It was one of the most important questions ever asked.

It was asked of Jesus in a time when he was being grilled with questions. They were trying to get him to answer one wrong. They asked him questions like:

"Should we pay taxes to another king if God is our King?"

"Who will you be married to in heaven if you were married more than once on earth?"

Tough questions for sure, but Jesus gave answer after answer that left them scratching their heads. He gave answers that they didn't expect. He gave answers that were filled with a truth that they had never encountered. But none of their questions were as important as the one asked that day by the expert in the law. It was the one they all wondered about. With page after page of rules and rules about rules, with scrolls and then scrolls about scrolls.

The question: "Which is the greatest commandment in the Law?"

Ha! Surely they had him now. Would he say, "Do not murder," and neglect to mention "Honor your father and mother"? Would he say, "You shall have no idols," and forget "Don't covet your neighbor's wife"?

They had him. There was no right answer. How could he give one answer saying one was more important than the other when they were all sacred? For the first time he would trip over his words.

Jesus took a deep breath as if to say "good question." He gathered his thoughts, but he didn't pause long. His answer echoes through the centuries.

> "Love the Lord your God with all your heart and all your soul and with all your mind."
>
> Matthew 22:37 (NIV)

Ah, not one of the Ten Commandments, but still found in the Law of Moses. Jesus shared a phrase every Jew would know. It would have been recited in their worship services as a part of the Shema. They had heard it a thousand times.

Just as they considered Jesus' answer, though, Jesus kept talking. He said, "This is the first and the greatest commandment. And the second is like it" (Matthew 22:38-39 NIV). They had only asked for one. They had only asked for the greatest. Jesus couldn't stop. There is another commandment that is so like the first that they go hand in hand. I will not give you just one.

"Love your neighbor as yourself."

Matthew 22:3

This one was a little more obscure. It is found in the Book of Leviticus (Leviticus 19:18) sandwiched in between dozens of other rules. It is right next to "don't mate different kinds of animals" and "don't wear cloth woven of two kinds of materials."

But to Jesus it was of almost equal importance to the first. He couldn't mention one without the other.

Love is the greatest thing we can do.

Love God. Love people.

For Jesus, everything hangs on love.

And his answer silenced the crowd.

This devotion will lead you deeper into the most important thing you can ever do: loving God and loving others. Loving large. Not just talking about it, but doing it. It will involve loving God with all your heart and all your soul and all your mind, and this love for God will be closely linked with loving people in a way that is like the way you love yourself.

Jesus wanted us to infuse our world with the love that we have received and learned from God. This kind of love can in fact change our world. So, in a world that seems to run on so many things (money, greed, oil, power, etc.), what would our world look like if it ran on love? This devotion will give real opportunities for you to love God and love your neighbor in the hopes of a changed you, a changed community, and a changed world.

You are invited to love God and love your neighbor in a way that changes—to love large.

How to Use
These Devotions

Be Still: It is recommended that you set aside a certain time and place each day to do your *Loving Large* devotion. Find a place where you can sit comfortably, but not so comfortable that you fall asleep! Once you are seated take a deep breath. Let the thoughts and worries of your day fade out of your mind. Don't rush the beginning of your time with God. Be still and allow your heart to open to God.

Pray: Once you have found a still place, you will begin with the simple prayer for the week found on the title page for each week. Read the prayer silently or aloud. The same prayer will be said each day of the week at the beginning and the end of your devotion time. This repetition will allow the theme for the week to sink into your heart and be carried with you throughout the day.

Read: Next is a selected passage of Scripture. The Scripture for the week is found on the title page for the week. Read the Scripture in its entirety.

Focus: Each day there will be a focus verse: a shorter passage for you to focus on for the day.

Read: Then you will find the devotional thought for each day. Read the reflection and consider how this Scripture intersects with your life today.

Write: Each day you will find reflection questions where you can write your thoughts or questions.

Pray: You are invited again to pray the prayer for that week.

Week 1:
The Distracted Life

Jesus, I hear you calling me to love God with everything I've got. I want to do that today in a way that changes me and changes my world. I hear you calling me to love my neighbor the way that I love myself. Help me to love myself more fully and to give love to all that I encounter today. In your name. Amen.

Matthew 22:34-40

When the Pharisees heard that Jesus had left the Sadducees speechless, they met together.

One of them, a legal expert, tested him. "Teacher, what is the greatest commandment in the Law?"

He replied, *"You must love the Lord your God with all your heart, with all your being,* and with all your mind.

This is the first and greatest commandment.

And the second is like it: *You must love your neighbor as you love yourself.* All the Law and the Prophets depend on these two commands.

Day 1

Matthew 22:34-36

When the Pharisees heard that Jesus had left the Sadducees speechless, they met together. One of them, a legal expert, tested him. "Teacher, what is the greatest commandment in the Law?"

I think it was the most important question ever asked.

The religious leaders were trying to trick Jesus, trying to trip him up with an unanswerable question. Jesus did not see this as a chance to prove his intelligence, his knowledge of the Law, or show his cleverness.

Jesus saw it as an opportunity to share with them what is truly important. In a life with many distractions, we can so easily run after things that are not of significance. Jesus' answer pointed them and us to what the heart was made to focus upon.

Loving God. And loving God large.

Before we examine Jesus' world-changing answer to the question "What is the greatest commandment in the Law?" I think it could be helpful to first consider what questions we have for God and our reasons for asking.

The religious leaders of his day seemed to be asking Jesus a trick question to prove to others that Jesus was a hoax.

Perhaps they asked because some really wondered of the true answer to this theological question. Perhaps some were hoping for an answer that could give life.

If Jesus was in your town today and you were afforded the chance to ask him a question, what would you ask?

What do you want to ask Jesus today?

What would be your motivation behind the question? Why would you ask this question(s)?

Jesus listened to and answered the questions of the people in his day. He is listening to you and wanting to give you an answer. The answer will always be love. He offers love to you and requires love from you.

Jesus, I hear you calling me to love God with everything I've got. I want to do that today in a way that changes me and changes my world. I hear you calling me to love my neighbor the way that I love myself. Help me to love myself more fully and to give love to all that I encounter today. In your name. Amen.

Day 2

Matthew 22:37-38

He replied, *"You must love the Lord your God with all your heart, with all your being,* and with all your mind. This is the first and greatest commandment."

Jesus' answer seems simple. It may seem obvious.

Some of us may even consider it revolutionary.

Religion has the tendency to become distracted. Not intentionally. In fact religion generally has very good intentions. However, we begin to make rules to keep us close to the heart of our religion. Then we make rules about those rules. Then people don't follow the rules, and there have to be punishments for those who break those rules. And then, without even noticing, the religion becomes about many human-made constructs that have little to do with what got the whole thing started in the first place.

Jesus had a way of cutting through all that with simple yet powerful statements that pointed people to the truth. His answer to a question that took into account hundreds of years of religion was simple, obvious, and powerful.

Love God. Love God with all your heart, soul, and mind. Love God with everything you've got.

We can sometimes more easily think of ways to show other people love than we can think of ways to love God.

What ways do you regularly love God?

The time you are taking today to read Scripture and pray as a part of this devotion is one way that you can be intentional with your time to love God.

How does taking intentional time to love God change the way you look at your day?

The most important thing you can do is love God. Don't push those intentional times off. Don't neglect to see how, even in the busyness of your day, your heart can be attuned to loving God.

Jesus, I hear you calling me to love God with everything I've got. I want to do that today in a way that changes me and changes my world. I hear you calling me to love my neighbor the way that I love myself. Help me to love myself more fully and to give love to all that I encounter today. In your name, Amen

Day 3

Matthew 22:39

And the second is like it: *You must love your neighbor as you love yourself.*

Jesus was asked to share his thoughts on the greatest commandment. What's number one? What's the most important? If we could only do one, which one?

Jesus answers by saying, "Love God with everything you've got," but he doesn't stop there. He keeps talking. For Jesus, you can't pause long between "Love God" and "Love neighbor." He says that the second is like the first one. They are connected. If you do the first one, don't neglect the second.

Samuel Clark is a ten-year-old in my church. A couple months before his birthday while looking at a magazine, Samuel saw a picture of boy his age in a faraway country that had a cleft palate. Samuel began to cry. He read about how without reconstructive surgery this boy's health was in great danger. Samuel asked his mom if he could use his birthday money to help a child with a cleft palate. I was with Samuel on the night of his birthday after he learned that he had raised enough money for five surgeries for five children. There was a look in his eyes that said, *Anything in the world is possible.* There was a large love in his eyes that inspired me to do more.

Oh, yeah I didn't tell you—I didn't have to. Samuel loves God. He loves God with everything he's got. His love for God and his love for neighbor are so closely connected that you can hardly tell them apart.

Jesus, when asked about how we should live, immediately told us to love God. He also knew that love would lead us to love others. Jesus was fed up with religious people who talked about a great love for God and who exhibited no compassion for their neighbors. According to Jesus, it just can't work that way.

How does your love for God affect how you treat others?

Who do you think you might be called upon to love today in a large way? Which neighbor?

The love that you have for God will directly inform and empower how you can love those around you today.

Jesus, I hear you calling me to love God with everything I've got. I want to do that today in a way that changes me and changes my world. I hear you calling me to love my neighbor the way that I love myself. Help me to love myself more fully and to give love to all that I encounter today. In your name. Amen.

Day 4

Matthew 22:40

All the Law and the Prophets depend on these two commands.

The news tells us that our world is in trouble. Nations are crumbling. Violence is on the rise. There are stacks of food in one country while people in another starve. The economy is on edge. We think everything is okay. Then the next breaking news hits the airwaves, and we no longer feel okay.

The world is described as unstable, volatile, greedy, and unjust. Here's what I think it is: distracted.

God made us to love and be loved.

When our world runs on money, power, oil, greed, or sex, then we are a world distracted. We were made to run on love.

Jesus said that everything hangs on just two things: loving God and loving neighbor. If we could get these two right, everything else would fall into place.

The world isn't a mistake; it wasn't thrown together haphazardly, but it is greatly distracted from its purpose: a people made by God and for God, made to love God and love each other.

What are your concerns for the world?

How do you think love might make a difference?

God puts the hope for a troubled world in our hands when he points us to the commands to love God and love neighbor.

How can God use you?

Jesus, I hear you calling me to love God with everything I've got. I want to do that today in a way that changes me and changes my world. I hear you calling me to love my neighbor the way that I love myself. Help me to love myself more fully and to give love to all that I encounter today. In your name. Amen.

Day 5

Mark 12:17

Jesus said to them, "Give to Caesar what belongs to Caesar and to God what belongs to God." His reply left them overcome with wonder.

We are easily distracted. A recent study indicates that the effects of technology and multi-tasking have contributed to an ever-lowering attention span.[1]

You weren't made to live a distracted life. You weren't made to have seventeen windows open at the same time, trying to attend to seventeen things at once and not doing any one thing well. You were actually made to live a focused life, a life focused on love.

Many of the people that were questioning Jesus were clearly distracted. They were in the presence of the Son of God and they asked him questions to test his knowledge of God's law. Rather than get to know him or enjoy him, they want him to do something for them.

One time they asked him a question about to whom they should pay taxes. They asked not because they truly wanted to know the answer, but instead because they wanted to trap Jesus in his words. They were distracted.

When Jesus answered such questions he always pointed them away from the technical question and toward the God who they needed to focus on.

If you were in the presence of Jesus, would you seek to know him and enjoy him or would you be too distracted to do so?

What are the big distractions in your life?

What would help you focus on your God given purpose (to love and be loved)?

Jesus, I hear you calling me to love God with everything I've got. I want to do that today in a way that changes me and changes my world. I hear you calling me to love my neighbor the way that I love myself. Help me to love myself more fully and to give love to all that I encounter today. In your name. Amen.

---

1. Lloyds TSB, "'Five-minute memory' costs Brits £1.6 billion," accessed August 16, 2013, http://www.insurance.lloydstsb.com/personal/general/mediacentre/homehazards_pr.asp.

Day 6

John 13:34

"I give you a new commandment: Love each other. Just as I have loved you, so you also must love each other.

Most of us agree with Jesus when he says loving others is of utmost importance. It is the way that he says we are to do it that we have the most trouble with.

Love your neighbor as yourself.

In a life full of distractions we often look at our neighbors and think about what they can do for us. Now, we wouldn't say that, but our actions show that we think it. We get frustrated with the checkout guy at the grocery. We are angry with other drivers on the interstate. We are rude with our family members. Why? Because we look to them and wonder what they can do for us. Get me through the line quickly, get out of my way on the road, do your share of the chores. The love that Jesus is talking about calls us to stop seeing others as a means to our ends, and look at others' needs as if they were our own.

Love others like you love yourself.

Some of us, though, have trouble loving ourselves. If you have trouble with this, Jesus has something to say to you too. To you, Jesus offers this command, "Love as I have loved you."

Both "loving neighbor as self" and "loving as Jesus has loved us" call us to lift others up and consider the needs of others. We don't see people as means to achieving what we need for the day. We see them like we see ourselves and love them fully and wholly. We see them the way Jesus sees them, so we serve them and care for them.

We love the checkout guy, and the driver on the road, and the brother in our house. We love them like we love ourselves. We love them the way Jesus loves us.

What do you think it would mean for you to love your neighbor as yourself?

What would it mean to love others the way Jesus loves you?

Jesus, I hear you calling me to love God with everything I've got. I want to do that today in a way that changes me and changes my world. I hear you calling me to love my neighbor the way that I love myself. Help me to love myself more fully and to give love to all that I encounter today. In your name. Amen.

Day 7

Revelation 2:4-5

But I have this against you: you have let go of the love you had at first. So remember the high point from which you have fallen. Change your hearts and lives and do the things you did at first. If you don't, I'm coming to you. I will move your lampstand from its place if you don't change your hearts and lives.

In the Book of Revelation, the church of Ephesus is told that they have let go of the love they had at first. Another way of saying this is that they had forgotten their first love.

Jesus says our first love should be God.

With all the things that pull at our hearts and clamor for attention, God has to come first. When God moves down the list to second, third, or fourth place, everything else gets messed up.

We must change our hearts and our lives. Another way of saying this is to repent.

If you look at your life and see that God is not in the rightful place of first, then take some time today and repent, change, and ask God for help.

What would you want to say to God about your desire to love

God first?

What do you need to repent of or change to put God first?

Loving Large will require a primary focus on God that will then spill out onto all of your other devotions and relationships. God desires this of you. God requires this of you.

Jesus, I hear you calling me to love God with everything I've got. I want to do that today in a way that changes me and changes my world. I hear you calling me to love my neighbor the way that I love myself. Help me to love myself more fully and to give love to all my neighbors. In your name. Amen.

Week 2:
Your Love Keeps
Lifting Me Higher

God, as I stop today to pray, I consider how extravagant your love is for me. You have sought me out and given so freely. You gave your son Jesus, so I could have life. Accept my thanks today. Show me how I can live a life that loves and gives in extravagant ways. In Jesus' name. Amen.

Song of Solomon 8:6-7

Set me as a seal over your heart,
  as a seal upon your arm,
for love is as strong as death,
  passionate love unrelenting as the grave.
Its darts are darts of fire—
  divine flame!
Rushing waters can't quench love;
  rivers can't wash it away.
If someone gave
  all his estate in exchange for love,
  he would be laughed to utter shame.

Day 1

Song of Solomon 4:1-2

Look at you—so beautiful, my dearest!
Look at you—so beautiful! Your eyes are doves
    behind the veil of your hair!
Your hair is like a flock of goats
    as they stream down Mount Gilead.
Your teeth are like newly shorn ewes
    as they come up from the washing pool—
    all of them perfectly matched,
    not one of them lacks its twin.

Found in the middle of our Bible, tucked in between the wisdom of Ecclesiastes and the prophecy of Isaiah, is a love song. We often call it a book, but even its title tells us it is something much different from that. The Song of Solomon is just that: a song written between Solomon the king and his beloved.

It is passionate, graphic, and moving. It is excessive at times. It is over the top.

It is no different than a more contemporary attempt by a musician to express his love for his lover. Love songs and romantic offerings are always over the top. The lover is trying to express a feeling in his heart that is hard to convey, so he uses exaggerated language and extravagant gifts.

People often wonder why Solomon's ancient love song is included in our Holy Scriptures. It says nothing of God, the Messiah, or prophecy. Why is it included then?

The answer seems to be that God would want us to know that there is an over-the-top, extravagant love that is pursuing us: the love of God.

Warning: When you begin to believe that God loves you in the radical kind of crazy, "I'll do anything" type of love that a lover has for her beloved, your life will never be the same. Some of us aren't even sure if God likes us! Some of us have great doubts that God would ever come close to us because of what we have done or where we have been. When you start to believe that God loves you in a pursuing love song kind of way, your life will never be the same.

Is it hard for you to believe that God loves you this way?

What hinders you from believing it?

God, as I stop today to pray, I consider how extravagant your love is for me. You have sought me out and given so freely. You gave your son Jesus, so I could have life. Accept my thanks today. Show me how I can live a life that loves and gives in extravagant ways. In Jesus' name. Amen.

Day 2

Song of Solomon 8:6a
> Set me as a seal over your heart,
>   as a seal upon your arm,

If this love song is also being sung to us, then God is asking us to place God like a seal over our hearts and as a seal on our arms.

What does this mean?

A seal signifies that something is authorized property or has authorized use. The seal tells others to whom something belongs.

If God's seal is on your heart it means that you belong to God. In Ephesians, Paul writes that "When you believed, you were marked in him with a seal, the promised Holy Spirit" (Ephesians 1:13b NIV). There could be no more powerful way that God could say, "You are mine," than by saying "I have sealed your heart."

The seal is also on our arms. It isn't just a "me and God" thing. It's on my sleeve for everyone to see.

Jesus said love God *and* love neighbor. Our love from God and our love for God should directly affect our love for others. The seal is on our hearts, and the seal is on our arm.

Solomon desired for his beloved to know that his love was in her heart. It was something that she carried with her that gave her joy and comfort. But he also desired for the seal to be on her arm. Others would know that she was in relationship with him.

God sings to us a love song of great love for us. We carry it with us in our hearts giving us joy and comfort. But the song is heard by others, and they are changed because of the love pouring out of our hearts for them.

Do you feel that your heart is sealed by God's love? What does this mean to you?

Do others see God's seal on your arm? How can you show them?

God, as I stop today to pray, I consider how extravagant your love is for me. You have sought me out and given so freely. You gave your son Jesus, so I could have life. Accept my thanks today. Show me how I can live a life that loves and gives in extravagant ways. In Jesus' name. Amen.

Day 3

Song of Solomon 8:6*b*

For love is as strong as death,
 passionate love unrelenting as the grave.

L ove with jealousy is not always a bad thing.

From time to time I will visit children in the hospital. Often their mothers and fathers may not even look at me during the entire visit. Their eyes are fixed on their child. Their hearts are fixed on their child. In the midst of these intense times, they are focused on protecting and advocating for their beloved one. Their love is jealous and unyielding.

Solomon's song here is often translated as saying my love's "jealousy [is] unyielding as the grave" (NIV). A pretty serious statement. Solomon is serious.

This week is about discovering that God's love is extravagant in its pursuit of you. God's love is also jealous. God's love is strong and unyielding.

You have no doubt that people let you down—people who you thought would be there for you and then they weren't. You expected their love to be there, and it wasn't. They yielded when you needed them to be steadfast.

People make promises, of course, that they can't always keep. God always keeps God's promises. God promises to be there with a love that protects and advocates for you. This promise is true. You can count on it.

How does life look different for you if you believe that God's love for you is unyielding (it's not going anywhere, no matter the circumstances)?

God, as I stop today to pray, I consider how extravagant your love is for me. You have sought me out and given so freely. You gave your son Jesus, so I could have life. Accept my thanks today. Show me how I can live a life that loves and gives in extravagant ways. In Jesus' name. Amen.

Day 4

Exodus 20:4-6

Do not make an idol for yourself—no form whatsoever—of anything in the sky above or on the earth below or in the waters under the earth. Do not bow down to them or worship them, because I, the LORD your God, am a jealous God. I punish children for their parents' sins even to the third and fourth generations of those who hate me. But I am loyal and gracious to the thousandth generation of those who love me and keep my commandments.

Yesterday, we considered what it might mean to have a God who jealously loves us. Jealousy doesn't have to be a negative if we consider that it speaks of a love that is strong and unyielding. In Exodus God proclaimed to be a jealous God who would not stand for God's children to worship other idols. In this case God's jealousy is like the jealousy we feel when someone we love gives his or her love to someone else in an unfaithful manner.

God's love is again calling us to a primary and singular devotion to God. Jesus said love God first, and then your love for others will flow from that love. Notice, though, how God describes to the Israelites the way that our love for God or lack thereof can affect others.

When we give our hearts to other idols it affects our families to the third and fourth generations. Our grandchildren and great-grandchildren are negatively affected when we give our hearts to gods other than God.

However, notice the effect we have on others when we do choose to love God in a faithful way. God says that a thousand generations are affected by those who seek and love God first (v. 6). The best thing we can do to leave a legacy is love God.

What kind of legacy do you want to leave? What does this verse say to you about what you can do to realize that?

God, as I stop today to pray, I consider how extravagant your love is for me. You have sought me out and given so freely. You gave your son Jesus, so I could have life. Accept my thanks today. Show me how I can live a life that loves and gives in extravagant ways. In Jesus' name. Amen.

Day 5

Song of Solomon 8:7-8

Rushing waters can't quench love;
   rivers can't wash it away.
If someone gave
   all his estate in exchange for love,
   he would be laughed to utter shame.

Solomon says if you were to exchange your whole estate for love you would be considered a fool. If you give everything up for love you should expect to be laughed at.

Is Solomon saying don't give up anything for love? No, he is saying you should give up everything for love, just be prepared for the backlash! His whole love song proclaims his willingness to be foolish and extravagant for the one that he loves. And who cares if you are scorned! Love is worth it.

What does this love song teach us about love?

God's love for you is extravagant.

Your love for God should be extravagant.

Your love for others should be extravagant. People will think you are crazy if you are extravagant, and don't worry about that. It is worth it.

What is God calling you to give away so that others will see your love for God?

How is God calling you to be extravagant in loving others?

Be ready for others to misunderstand this love. Be ready for others to misunderstand you. Don't worry about it; it will be worth it.

God, as I stop today to pray, I consider how extravagant your love is for me. You have sought me out and given so freely. You gave your son Jesus, so I could have life. Accept my thanks today. Show me how I can live a life that loves and gives in extravagant ways. In Jesus' name. Amen.

Day 6

John 12:3

Then Mary took an extraordinary amount, almost three-quarters of a pound, of very expensive perfume made of pure nard. She anointed Jesus' feet with it, then wiped his feet dry with her hair. The house was filled with the aroma of the perfume.

When Mary anointed Jesus feet with an expensive perfume, it could have been described in a number of ways.

Extravagant. Wasteful. Foolish.

One of Jesus' disciples even described it as unfaithful. The perfume could have been sold and the money given to the poor.

Remember that when love is extravagantly given, there will be criticism. Mary didn't seem to care. She loved Jesus, and like writing an over-the-top love song, she gave an over-the-top gift. Her heart demanded her to do so and it had a great effect on all who saw it. We are still talking about it today.

When you hear about Mary's extravagant gift, how does it make you feel?

God's love leads us to love large, to give extravagantly, and sometimes when you do this, you will feel great hesitation. Why? It may seem wasteful or even foolish. The Mary story encourages us to follow our hearts and do extravagant things that lead people to consider who Jesus must really be for someone to do something like that.

God will place before you an opportunity to show God's love in an extravagant way. Prepare for it. Ask God to give you the courage to take the risk and be a part of it. Then, people will hear about it and be pointed to a God who gives and loves extravagantly.

God, as I stop today to pray, I consider how extravagant your love is for me. You have sought me out and given so freely. You gave your son Jesus, so I could have life. Accept my thanks today. Show me how I can live a life that loves and gives in extravagant ways. In Jesus' name. Amen.

Day 7

John 3:16

God so loved the world that he gave his only Son, so that everyone who believes in him won't perish but will have eternal life.

Some of us have heard John 3:16 so many times that we hardly even think about its meaning when we do. Some of us are only familiar with the reference as we have seen it on a poster board at sporting events.

Either way, it is worth spending some time on it. We hear in it Jesus' concise explanation of what is the most extravagant gift ever.

God gave his Son.

I'll let that sink in for a moment.

God gave his Son.

The one thing that most of us would not give up, God was willing to give. Why?

Love.

God loved the world so much that God gave his Son. God did this so we could know life.

We see this gift most extravagantly expressed when Jesus died on the cross. In this sacrificial act our sins were forgiven, and we were offered life eternally.

Take a moment to express your thanks to God for this indescribable gift.

As we reflect on it we see our expressions of love only as thank offerings to a God who gave everything for us. We realize that in our lives we have opportunity to sacrifice and give, so others can know this great love. Jesus says there is nothing more important that we can do than offer our love for God and offer God's love to others.

God, as I stop today to pray, I consider how extravagant your love is for me. You have sought me out and given so freely. You gave your son Jesus, so I could have life. Accept my thanks today. Show me how I can live a life that loves and gives in extravagant ways. In Jesus' name. Amen.

Week 3:
Loving Is Giving

O God, my heart often feels divided. My desire today is for my heart to be centered on you. Guide me today toward a life that is more focused on loving you and loving people. My treasure is in you. In Jesus' name. Amen.

Matthew 6:19-24

"Stop collecting treasures for your own benefit on earth, where moth and rust eat them and where thieves break in and steal them. Instead, collect treasures for yourselves in heaven, where moth and rust don't eat them and where thieves don't break in and steal them. Where your treasure is, there your heart will be also.

"The eye is the lamp of the body. Therefore, if your eye is healthy, your whole body will be full of light. But if your eye is bad, your whole body will be full of darkness. If then the light in you is darkness, how terrible that darkness will be! No one can serve two masters. Either you will hate the one and love the other, or you will be loyal to the one and have contempt for the other. You cannot serve God and wealth."

Day 1

Matthew 6:19-20

"Stop collecting treasures for your own benefit on earth, where moth and rust eat them and where thieves break in and steal them. Instead, collect treasures for yourselves in heaven, where moth and rust don't eat them and where thieves don't break in and steal them.

Like many kids, when I was young, I collected baseball cards. I had shoeboxes filled with them. My most prized cards were sealed in plastic cases to protect them. I spent hours studying them, enjoying them, and considering their value.

What do you collect?

While I'm sure Jesus was not addressing the types of collections we have for our hobbies in these verses, He was asking us to consider what we are spending hours studying, enjoying, and giving value to. Jesus knew that many of the things we store up here on earth will eventually decay and rust. They are temporary. Jesus was also inviting us to be a part of collecting treasures that have eternal value, the type of thing that no moth or rust or thief here on earth can touch.

What do you think Jesus was talking about when he suggested we collect treasures in heaven?

Are there any treasures on earth that you feel you need to stop collecting?

Jesus does not want us to give up earthly pleasures as much as he welcomes us into a life that can have eternal worth. This life is found in giving ourselves, as fully as we know how, to loving God and to loving our neighbors.

O God, my heart often feels divided. My desire today is for my heart to be centered on you. Guide me today toward a life that is more focused on loving you and loving people. My treasure is in you. In Jesus' name. Amen.

Day 2

Matthew 6:21

Where your treasure is, there your heart will be also.

Most of us, if asked to name the top two or three most important things in our lives, could give a pretty quick answer. A different question, though, would be to name where we spend the majority of our time, money, and energy. If people were to examine your calendar, your to-do list, and your personal budget, would they see that the things you most value receive the most of your time, your energy, and your money?

Jesus said that where your treasure is there your heart will be also. Not that your treasure will follow your heart, but that your heart will follow your treasure. This means we must examine and be intentional about what we are giving ourselves to, where our treasure is going.

Where do you desire to be giving your time, money, and energy?

If someone were to objectively observe your life, what do you think they would say is your "treasure"?

We often experience a disconnect between what we *want* to give our lives to and what we *should* give our lives to. This does not mean that we are stuck there. It does mean that you may have to take some steps in re-prioritizing where you are spending your time, energy, and money. Your heart will follow your treasure.

Jesus is concerned about our treasure because Jesus is concerned about our hearts. He knows that if you give yourself to ungodly pursuits for an extended period of time, your heart will be affected.

What can you do today to give your heart to God?

O God, my heart often feels divided. My desire today is for my heart to be centered on you. Guide me today toward a life that is more focused on loving you and loving people. My treasure is in you. In Jesus' name. Amen.

Day 3

Matthew 6:24

No one can serve two masters. Either you will hate the one and love the other, or you will be loyal to the one and have contempt for the other. You cannot serve God and wealth.

Bob Dylan wrote a song in the late 1970s entitled "Gotta Serve Somebody." In it Dylan writes, "It may be the devil or it may be the Lord / But you're gonna have to serve somebody."[1] Dylan wasn't putting service to God and the devil on the same level, but he was saying we all serve somebody or something, and it would be better to choose whom you serve rather than find yourself inadvertently serving one that you did not choose. I think he also was lifting up the fact that you can't serve both. It is one or the other.

Long before Dylan, Jesus talked about the difficulty in serving two masters. Jesus also thought it better to choose what (or whom) you would serve rather than letting it choose you.

No one, Jesus said, can serve two masters. He warns that we can easily serve our desire to have wealth, to accumulate earthly treasure, and neglect our heart's purpose, which is to love and serve God.

Does your heart ever feel divided? If so, what is it divided between?

In what ways do you find yourself to be self-serving right now?

You were made not to make a bunch of money, to accumulate a bunch of stuff, or to make your name great. You were created to love God and love people. Loving God and loving people mean serving God and serving others. Often the way we serve God is by serving others. You will find your heart at peace when it is focused on God and used for the purposes of God.

What can you do today to serve God by serving God's people?

O God, my heart often feels divided. My desire today is for my heart to be centered on you. Guide me today toward a life that is more focused on loving you and loving people. My treasure is in you. In Jesus' name. Amen.

---

1. Bob Dylan, "Gotta Serve Somebody," in *Slow Train Coming*, Special Rider Music, 1979.

Day 4

Acts 20:35

In everything I have shown you that, by working hard, we must help the weak. In this way we remember the Lord Jesus' words: 'It is more blessed to give than to receive.'"

The saying "it is more blessed to give than to receive" has become a part of popular culture. I remember hearing it as a child, and I must admit I received it with more than just a little skepticism. This was something parents told their kids, I thought, to lessen their disappointment about not getting good gifts. It was one of those tricks that parents use like "Eat your vegetables" and "Go to bed early." It wasn't true, but it benefited them somehow.

It wasn't until much later that I learned that this was one of the sayings of Jesus remembered by his early followers.

Jesus really thought there was more blessing in giving than getting?

Yes, he did.

Jesus taught us to love God and love neighbor. Those that love also give, and those that give experience great blessing.

Blessing is often defined as happiness, and though God's blessing is surely more than happiness, happiness is a good place to start.

There is a happiness that cannot be experienced in receiving or taking that can only be found in giving. Jesus was concerned about the condition of our hearts, and he knew that we would experience more happiness of heart if we were giving.

Here in Acts the emphasis is on giving to the weak. We work hard to give to help the weak.

Who will you encounter today that is weak?

What can you give to show them God's love?

O God, my heart often feels divided. My desire today is for my heart to be centered on you. Guide me today toward a life that is more focused on loving you and loving people. My treasure is in you. In Jesus' name. Amen.

Day 5

Matthew 16:25

All who want to save their lives will lose them. But all who lose their lives because of me will find them.

A paradox is a statement that at first seems contradictory or against common sense and yet holds great truth.

Jesus was big on paradoxes.

We looked yesterday at one paradox from Acts where Jesus is quoted as saying "it is more blessed to give than to receive." At first glance, we say "Huh? Surely it is more blessed to receive than to give something away?" Jesus urges us to look again, and we realize that there is indeed more blessing in giving than receiving.

Here in Matthew 16, Jesus throws another paradox our way. He proposes that if we want to save our lives, we will first have to lose our life.

Huh?

Surely, I read that wrong.

Look again: "All who want to save their lives will lose them. But all who lose their lives because of me will find them." If we want to find life, we will give up our lives for Jesus.

So, what does it mean to lose your life because of Jesus? It means that we would be willing to love large, to love with everything we've got, to love God first and foremost and be willing to love our neighbors like we love ourselves. When you love God with all your heart, mind, and strength, you give up your life. When you love your neighbor as you love yourself, you lose a lot. And in losing, you find so much more. You actually find life in giving up your life for God and others.

There are many ways to lose your life. The loss that Jesus is proposing is much different than losing yourself in co-dependence or chemical dependence. It is much different from losing your life to a job that demands your soul and every minute of your day.

Jesus is saying lose your life by giving it to me and by giving it for others. When you love like that, you find life.

How have you experienced loss that has actually been gain for you?

O God, my heart often feels divided. My desire today is for my heart to be centered on you. Guide me today toward a life that is more focused on loving you and loving people. My treasure is in you. In Jesus' name. Amen.

Day 6

Psalm 24:1

> The earth is the LORD's and everything in it,
>   the world and its inhabitants too.

Loving is giving. Giving, though, is often hard for us because we forget one central truth of the Scriptures.

Everything belongs to God.

The earth is the Lord's and everything in it.

When I clutch tightly to the things that are mine, I forget that everything belongs to God.

When I feel that the world revolves around me, I forget that the earth is the Lord's.

When I am consumed with worry for the people that I love, I forget that all the inhabitants of the world belong to God.

When I am reluctant to give away what I have for fear of what will be left in my hands, I forget that the earth is the Lord's and everything in it.

Unfortunately, I forget a lot.

Fortunately, God remembers my forgetful nature and reminds me in so many loving and gentle ways.

Remember today that God is calling you to love and to give. When you begin to clutch tightly to things that aren't really yours, remember that you and all you hold belong to God.

What are you holding tightly today that you need to be reminded actually belongs to God?

What does it mean to you that you belong to God?

O God, my heart often feels divided. My desire today is for my heart to be centered on you. Guide me today toward a life that is more focused on loving you and loving people. My treasure is in you. In Jesus' name. Amen.

Day 7

Malachi 3:10

Bring the whole tenth-part to the storage house so there might be food in my house.

Please test me in this,

says the LORD of heavenly forces.

See whether I do not open all the windows of the heavens for you

and empty out a blessing until there is enough.

Loving is giving. This verse from Malachi is often used when talking about giving financially to the church. It forms much of the basis for many Christians' belief that one should tithe or give ten percent of their income to the church.

There is, though, more here than just a word about financial giving. This Scripture is about love. It is about a love for God that would allow you to place your whole trust in God's provision for your life. How do you place this trust? You give significantly to God.

You give your heart.

You give your life.

You give your money.

You give your time.

You give to God in a way that makes you vulnerable and totally reliant upon God.

God says, "Test me in this." It is rare that God asks for this kind of test. If you take the test, God promises to open all the windows of heaven and empty out a blessing onto you until there is enough. Let that sink in for a moment.

Are you ready to test God in this by giving sacrificially? What would this look like for you?

As you have given to God, how have you already experienced God's blessing and provision?

O God, my heart often feels divided. My desire today is for my heart to be centered on you. Guide me today toward a life that is more focused on loving you and loving people. My treasure is in you. In Jesus' name. Amen.

Week 4:
Can We Really
Change the World?

O God, I know that life is precious and life is short. I desire to live for you, give to you, and serve you. I know that your love for me is not dependent on what I do, and yet I desire to be a part of what you are calling me to do. Help me to see the unique things that you have for me. I will faithfully go wherever you call me. In Jesus' name. Amen.

Mark 12:28-34

One of the legal experts heard their dispute and saw how well Jesus answered them. He came over and asked him, "Which commandment is the most important of all?"

Jesus replied, "The most important one is *Israel, listen! Our God is the one Lord, and you must love the Lord your God with all your heart, with all your being, with all your mind, and with all your strength.* The second is this, *You will love your neighbor as yourself.* No other commandment is greater than these."

The legal expert said to him, "Well said, Teacher. You have truthfully said that God is one and there is no other besides him. And to love God with all of the heart, a full understanding, and all of one's strength, and to love one's neighbor as oneself is much more important than all kinds of entirely burned offerings and sacrifices."

When Jesus saw that he had answered with wisdom, he said to him, "You aren't far from God's kingdom." After that, no one dared to ask him any more questions.

Day 1

Mark 12:28-31

One of the legal experts heard their dispute and saw how well Jesus answered them. He came over and asked him, "Which commandment is the most important of all?" Jesus replied, "The most important one is *Israel, listen! Our God is the one Lord, and you must love the Lord your God with all your heart, with all your being, with all your mind, and with all your strength.* The second is this, *You will love your neighbor as yourself.* No other commandment is greater than these."

We have already spent some time with Matthew's account of Jesus answering the "what is most important" question. Here Mark tells a similar version.

Again, Jesus is asked the question, and again Jesus can't give just one answer. Again, Jesus connects our love for God with our love for neighbor. Why would it be necessary to spend another week on the same question and the same answer?

In Matthew, Jesus tells us that all the law and all the prophets hang on these two commandments. Here in Mark he simply says that "no other commandment is greater than these." If we can get these two things right, everything else falls into place.

This week we will consider how our love for God can lead us to be a part of changing our worlds and the world as people who love our neighbors.

First, this question: What comes more natural for you, loving God or loving others? Why do you think this is true?

List some ways you regularly show love for God.

List some ways you regularly show love for others.

Ask God to help you in the areas where you find it difficult to love.

Ask God to show you how you can be used to change the world simply by loving God and loving neighbor.

O God, I know that life is precious and life is short. I desire to live for you, give to you, and serve you. I know that your love for me is not dependent on what I do, and yet I desire to be a part of what you are calling me to do. Help me to see the unique things that you have for me. I will faithfully go wherever you call me. In Jesus' name. Amen.

Day 2

Mark 12:32-33

The legal expert said to him, "Well said, Teacher. You have truthfully said that God is one and there is no other besides him. And to love God with all of the heart, a full understanding, and all of one's strength, and to love one's neighbor as oneself is much more important than all kinds of entirely burned offerings and sacrifices."

The legal expert agreed with Jesus. Then, he brought up an interesting thought as it regards loving God and loving others. He said that to love God with all of your heart and to love one's neighbor are much more important than offering and sacrifices. Sure, Jesus had said these commandments were the most important things that you could do, but this clarification took it even deeper. The legal expert acknowledged that what Jesus was saying would cause religious people to look differently at their typical offering and sacrifices given in worship.

He doesn't say offerings and sacrifices are without merit; he just says that love is way more important. Burned offerings and sacrifices were the customary ways that people showed their devotion and faithfulness to God.

What do you think are some modern-day "burned offerings and sacrifices"? What are the expected and traditional things we do in worship that may not be as important as loving God and loving neighbor?

Maybe you mentioned church attendance, financial giving, or service to the church. Jesus would not say those things are without importance. He would say that these things must begin with love for God and love for neighbor, or they are worth little.

Are there some things that you are currently doing "for God" that are not connected to a deep love for God and love for people?

O God, I know that life is precious and life is short. I desire to live for you, give to you, and serve you. I know that your love for me is not dependent on what I do, and yet I desire to be a part of what you are calling me to do. Help me to see the unique things that you have for me. I will faithfully go wherever you call me. In Jesus' name. Amen.

Day 3

Mark 14:7

> You always have the poor with you; and whenever you want, you can do something good for them. But you won't always have me.

In Week 2, we remembered a time when one of Jesus' friends poured out an expensive perfume and washed Jesus feet with it. We marveled at this extravagant gift. Jesus was immediately criticized for allowing someone to be so excessive and wasteful. Jesus answered this criticism in a peculiar way.

He said, "You always have the poor with you" (v. 7a).

Many take this to believe that no matter what effort we take we will always have those among us who live in poverty. It has been two thousand years since Jesus made this statement, and even with our best efforts we have never been able to eradicate the world of poverty.

Does this mean Jesus doesn't care about the poor? Of course not. A careful examination of the life of Jesus finds that Jesus was constantly interacting with and serving people in need.

When Jesus announced his ministry he said it would be good news for the poor. Everything about Jesus says if we are not working with and loving those who are less fortunate than us economically, then we are missing the point of what it means to follow him.

So which is it? Is it "The poor will always be with us," or is it "Do everything you can to serve and love them?" The answer: Yes. The poor will always be with us and we are to do everything we can to take care of them.

Jesus has an ultimate anti-poverty plan that will be come to fruition when Christ returns to earth. Until then, as the people who love God we are called to love others in radical and extravagant ways.

Every Christian should consider what he or she is doing to change the world for the poor among us.

What is God calling you to do for the poor in your community and world?

O God, I know that life is precious and life is short. I desire to live for you, give to you, and serve you. I know that your love for me is not dependent on what I do, and yet I desire to be a part of what you are calling me to do. Help me to see the unique things that you have for me. I will faithfully go wherever you call me. In Jesus' name. Amen.

Day 4

Matthew 25:37-40

"Then those who are righteous will reply to him, 'Lord, when did we see you hungry and feed you, or thirsty and give you a drink? When did we see you as a stranger and welcome you, or naked and give you clothes to wear? When did we see you sick or in prison and visit you?'

"Then the king will reply to them, 'I assure you that when you have done it for one of the least of these brothers and sisters of mine, you have done it for me.'"

The first part of the greatest commandment is given first for a reason. Loving God with everything we've got is the first and most important part. We often wonder, though, *How can I show my love to God?*

Worship, prayer, and adoration are all ways that we can express that love, but sometimes we long for some tangible way that we can express our love to God. I think this is one of the reasons that Jesus connects the greatest commandment with the second one: to love your neighbor as yourself. Jesus is saying that one way we show love for God is by loving God's children.

In Matthew 25, we see this spelled out more clearly. After Jesus tells the righteous ones that they have fed him, given him drink, welcomed, clothed, and visited him, they ask, "When did we do that?!" Jesus is saying that they have shown love to him in very real and tangible ways, and they are left wondering when in the world did they do that!

Jesus says they did it when they love and served those who were in need. When they fed their hungry neighbor, they fed Jesus. When they welcomed the stranger, they welcomed Jesus. When they visited the prisoner, they visited Jesus.

If you want to fulfill the first commandment to love God, then you will fulfill the second to love your neighbor. When you love others, you express your love to God!

How are you loving God by loving your neighbors?

How might the realization that we can love God *by* loving our neighbors change the interactions you will have with others today? Will you do anything differently?

O God, I know that life is precious and life is short. I desire to live for you, give to you, and serve you. I know that your love for me is not dependent on what I do, and yet I desire to be a part of what you are calling me to do. Help me to see the unique things that you have for me. I will faithfully go wherever you call me. In Jesus' name. Amen.

Day 5

Mark 12:34

When Jesus saw that he had answered with wisdom, he said to him, "You aren't far from God's kingdom." After that, no one dared to ask him any more questions.

Jesus talked about the kingdom of God. A lot. Perhaps more than anything else Jesus talked about God's kingdom. He talked about God's kingdom being near, God's kingdom being here, and God's kingdom coming soon.

I would guess that you, like me, want to be close to God's kingdom. Not far, but oh, so close. I would love for it to be said of me, "You aren't far from God's kingdom."

What made Jesus say this about the legal expert?

He simply affirmed Jesus answer to the question about what is greatest. He agreed with Jesus that love for God with all of the heart and love for neighbor as oneself is more important than any offering or sacrifice.

In God's kingdom, God is the king, and love is the rule.

What kingdoms do you live in? What kings do you serve?

Do you feel that you are far from God's kingdom? If so, how?

As we learn in the Lord's Prayer, asking for God's "kingdom come" involves asking God's will to be done. Often, even though we desire to be close to God's kingdom, we also want what we want to happen. Living a life that loves large involves submitting yourself to God's will and seeing God's kingdom come on earth as it is in heaven.

O God, I know that life is precious and life is short. I desire to live for you, give to you, and serve you. I know that your love for me is not dependent on what I do, and yet I desire to be a part of what you are calling me to do. Help me to see the unique things that you have for me. I will faithfully go wherever you call me. In Jesus' name. Amen.

Day 6

1 Corinthians 13:13 (NIV)

And now these three remain: faith, hope, and love. But the greatest of these is love.

You may have heard this verse recited at a wedding or two. It follows a beautiful description of love, a love that is not rude or easily angered. Love is described as always protecting, trusting, hoping, and persevering. Paul says, "Love never fails" (1 Corinthians 13:8a).

This famous description of love, though, is not only or even primarily about the love that should be found between a man and woman in marriage. It is actually a description of the greatest gift of God's Spirit. We are told that above all things, love is the greatest gift that God gives us.

This devotional has been a focus on God's large love for us, the love we have for God, and the close connection between these two loves and our love for people. Hopefully it has been a time where you have considered how you can more fully live a life of love.

Knowing that God gives love as a gift of the Spirit, today

you are invited to spend a few moments asking God to give you love in certain areas of your life. You are also encouraged to think about what God's love would look like in these areas.

Ask God to give you love for the people in your family. What differences could God's love being shown through you make in your family?

Ask God to give you love for those you work and interact with each day. What differences could God's love being shown through you make in your everyday interactions with them?

Ask God to give you love for those you serve and worship with at your church. What differences could God's love being shown through you make in your church?

Ask God to give you love for those you dislike and those who have hurt you. What differences could a love for these people make in your heart and to these people?

O God, I know that life is precious and life is short. I desire to live for you, give to you, and serve you. I know that your love for me is not dependent on what I do, and yet I desire to be a part of what you are calling me to do. Help me to see the unique things that you have for me. I will faithfully go wherever you call me. In Jesus' name. Amen.

Day 7

1 John 4:19

We love because God first loved us.

When I was young, I learned a song that touched my heart. It is always with me. I will never forget it. Perhaps you learned the same one.

"Jesus loves me! This I know, for the Bible tells me so. / Little ones to him belong; they are weak, but he is strong. / Yes, Jesus loves me! Yes, Jesus loves me! / Yes, Jesus loves me! The Bible tells me so."[1]

Loving large has in many ways focused on how your love for God and neighbor can change the world. God desires to use you to share the greatest love with people who desperately need it. You have been challenged to consider how you can more fully live a life of love in intentional and specific ways. However, as we end today, we must be reminded that:

We love because God loved first.

We are little and weak, but the strong Jesus offers us love.

Without God's love for us, our desire to love in large and extravagant ways is impossible. We love because we have been loved by God.

Can you recall a time when you felt especially loved by God?

As we close, write a letter of thanks to God for the great love God has for you expressed in so many ways and expressed through Jesus Christ.

O God, I know that life is precious and life is short. I desire to live for you, give to you, and serve you. I know that your love for me is not dependent on what I do, and yet I desire to be a part of what you are calling me to do. Help me to see the unique things that you have for me. I will faithfully go wherever you call me. In Jesus' name. Amen.

---

1. Anna B. Warner, "Jesus Loves Me," *The United Methodist Hymnal* (Nashville: The United Methodist Publishing House, 1989), 191.